Sandra Day O'Connor

Sandra Day O'Connor receives an honorary law degree from the University of Minnesota Law School in 1987.

JUNIOR ▪ WORLD ▪ BIOGRAPHIES

Sandra Day O'Connor

NORMAN L. MACHT

CHELSEA JUNIORS

a division of CHELSEA HOUSE PUBLISHERS

Chelsea House Publishers
EDITOR-IN-CHIEF: Remmel Nunn
MANAGING EDITOR: Karyn Gullen Browne
COPY CHIEF: Mark Rifkin
PICTURE EDITOR: Adrian G. Allen
ART DIRECTOR: Maria Epes
ASSISTANT ART DIRECTOR: Howard Brotman
MANUFACTURING DIRECTOR: Gerald Levine
SYSTEMS MANAGER: Lindsey Ottman
PRODUCTION MANAGER: Joseph Romano
PRODUCTION COORDINATOR: Marie Claire Cebrián

JUNIOR WORLD BIOGRAPHIES

SENIOR EDITOR: Kathy Kuhtz

Staff for SANDRA DAY O'CONNOR
ASSOCIATE EDITOR: Wendy Murray
COPY EDITOR: Ian Wilker
EDITORIAL ASSISTANT: Karen Akins
PICTURE RESEARCHER: Ellen Barrett
SENIOR DESIGNER: Marjorie Zaum
COVER ILLUSTRATION: Vilma Ortiz

3 5 7 9 8 6 4 2

Library of Congress Cataloging-in-Publication Data
Macht, Norman L. (Norman Lee)
  Sandra Day O'Connor/Norman Macht.
    p. cm.—(Junior world biographies)
  Includes index.
  Summary: A biography of the first woman to be appointed as a justice of
the United States Supreme Court, giving background on her earlier legal
career.
  ISBN 0-7910-1756-7
  1. O'Connor, Sandra Day, 1930–   —Juvenile literature. 2. Judges—
United States—Biography—Juvenile literature. [1. O'Connor, Sandra Day,
1930–   . 2. United States. Supreme Court—Biography. 3. Judges.]
I. Title. II. Series.
KF8745.O25M33 1992
347.73'2634—dc20
[B]   91-22170
[347.3073534]   CIP
[B]   AC

Contents

Sandra Day O'Connor greets well-wishers after her confirmation in 1981. With her are (left to right) Attorney General William French Smith, Senator Barry Goldwater, Vice-president George Bush, and Senator Strom Thurmond.

1

A New Job

Going to work on the first day of a new job is always exciting, but often a little scary, too. It is something like the first day at a new school. The building is unfamiliar, and there are many people to meet and names to remember. No one knows what to expect from one another.

When Sandra Day O'Connor went to her new job on Monday, September 28, 1981, she did not know exactly what kinds of challenges she would face. Three days earlier she had been sworn in as an associate justice of the U.S. Supreme Court, the highest court in the nation. It was a job no woman had ever held before. All of the 101 justices, or judges, who had gone before her, including the 8 justices with whom she would be working, were men.

In addition to serving with the other justices, O'Connor would be in charge of a staff of secretaries and law clerks who would help her with her work. She would have to learn her way around the many offices and conference rooms in the Court building. It would take some time to become familiar with how the system worked, to get used to being trailed by security officers, and to establish a rapport, or working relationship, with the other justices. She also had to find a place to live and get accustomed to driving on the maze-like streets of Washington, D.C.

It was sunny but windy, with the temperature in the 60s, when O'Connor arrived at the imposing white-marble Supreme Court building that September morning. She was not surprised to find reporters and TV camera crews waiting for her in the driveway. Ever since July, when she had been nominated to the Supreme Court position by President Ronald Reagan, her world had turned into a media circus. Wherever she went, flashbulbs flared, and radio, newspaper, and television reporters crowded about, firing what seemed like a million questions at her. In her house in Phoenix, Arizona, where she lived with her husband and three sons, the telephone rang constantly. Her home had become about as private as a fish tank.

Anyone who is chosen for a high public position draws immediate media attention. But to be the first to do something is especially exciting. As they had done with the likes of Amelia Earhart, the first woman to fly a plane solo across the Atlantic Ocean, photographers followed Sandra Day O'Connor around as though she were royalty.

Before her Supreme Court appointment, O'Connor had been a judge and, before that, the first woman *majority leader* in the Arizona *legislature*, so she was used to seeing her picture in the newspapers and on television. But it is one thing to be a big fish in a small pond and something else to be suddenly just about the biggest fish in the whole world.

There has never been any law against women being on the Supreme Court. It was a tradition, however, to appoint men only. The custom was backed by the belief—held mostly by men—that such a technical, challenging job was too much for a woman to handle.

The nine justices of the Supreme Court deal with the most difficult and important legal questions, deciding what the nation's laws really mean. Their decisions have far-reaching effects and help shape American life. For example, the nation's schools are now racially integrated just because the Supreme Court declared school *segregation* by race *unconstitutional*. Similarly, Supreme Court decisions declared that public schools cannot require students to salute the flag or pray and that school boards cannot remove books from libraries just because they do not like the ideas presented in them.

Being the first woman to be appointed to a position of such influence is a great honor. But it is also "a Godawful burden," said a female college dean at the time of O'Connor's nomination. "She knows that she is going to have to prove, prove, prove."

O'Connor knew that she would be held to very high standards. Everything she said and did would be closely watched. She felt a special responsibility to do a good job so that it would be easier for other women to follow in her footsteps. She had the support of her family and the maturity, confidence, and honesty to be herself, regardless of what the world expected of her.

Throughout her dozens of interviews in the summer of 1981, including three days of tough questioning before a *U.S. Senate* committee, O'Connor was asked to give her opinions on many issues that might come before the Court.

O'Connor makes a point during her confirmation hearings while her husband and son listen intently at her side. The Senate committee asked O'Connor many difficult questions about law to see if she would be a suitable Supreme Court justice.

She would not say how she might vote on certain controversial or sensitive issues such as a woman's right to an abortion, and that made some people angry with her. It seemed there was no way she could avoid criticism, no matter what she said.

Some people wanted her to show that a woman justice would make a difference; some wanted her to prove that it would make no difference. "She should think like a woman," some said. "She should think like a man," said others.

O'Connor came to the conclusion that "it's not possible to satisfy everyone in this job." Nevertheless, she managed to satisfy the members of the U.S. Senate, who voted 99–0 to approve her appointment.

Sitting in her spacious office 10 years later, looking out at the Capitol, Sandra Day O'Connor remembered the awe she had felt that first day on the job. As she parked her car in the garage beneath the Supreme Court building, she had felt "a sense of wonder that someone who started out life as a child on a cattle ranch in southeastern Arizona would ever wind up as a member of the United States Supreme Court."

Sandra Day was eight years old when this photograph was taken. By then, she could brand cattle, drive a tractor, and shoot a rifle.

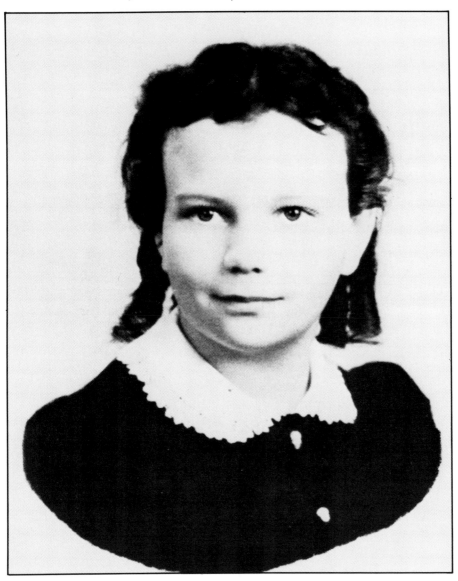

2

Life at the Lazy B Ranch

Sandra Day O'Connor was born in El Paso, Texas, on March 26, 1930. She was the first child of Ada Mae and Harry Day, who ran a huge cattle ranch on the Arizona–New Mexico border.

The ranch had been in the family since 1880, when Sandra's paternal grandfather, Henry Clay ("H. C.") Day, had bought 300 square miles of desert and grazing land in the Arizona Territory and stocked it with 5,000 cattle from Mexico. At that time, anyone who was willing to settle in the dusty, barren country of the Southwest could buy land from the federal government for very little money.

H. C. Day's cattle had been branded with a slanting *B*, called a "lazy" *B*, so he named his property the Lazy B ranch. (In 1912, when Arizona and New Mexico became states, their borderline ran right through the middle of the ranch.)

H. C. Day and his wife, Alice, lived in California and relied on a foreman to run the ranch. But the man turned out to be a cattle rustler who stole the cattle by putting his own brand on them. So the Days decided to move to the ranch and manage it themselves. H.C. and the cowboys who worked for him built a small adobe (sun-dried clay) house and planted orchards. It took a while for the Days to get used to the dusty, dry land, the unpredictable weather, and the fact that there were no neighbors for miles around.

The Days also had to deal with surprise visits from the Apache Indians who camped in the area. Like other American Indian peoples, the Apaches were angry at having been pushed off their ancestral land by the white settlers. Led by

Geronimo, they raided the Lazy B ranch from time to time, taking some horses and cows.

But despite the hazards of their frontier existence, the Days loved the ranch and the rugged, satisfying life it offered. As one of their descendants put it many years later, "This dried-up old piece of land is what we are."

When H. C. Day died in the early 1920s, his youngest son, Harry, took over the ranch. One day Harry traveled 200 miles to El Paso to buy cattle from a dealer named Willis Wilson Wilkey. There he met Wilkey's daughter, Ada Mae, who had recently graduated from the University of Arizona. They fell in love and were married in 1927.

Ada Mae had been raised in the city, but she quickly adapted to the more primitive way of life on the ranch. The Days had no electricity or running water in the house. Ada Mae pumped water from the well and did the cooking and cleaning for her husband and the four cowboys who worked on the ranch. She kept up with the world by subscribing to newspapers and magazines, and she owned many books.

The Days cooked their meals on a wood-burning stove and warmed a big kettle of water to take a bath. For heat they used a fireplace and an oil heater that ran all winter. A cake of ice kept food cold in the icebox.

H. C. Day had left some debts, and the young couple had very little money. About the time Sandra was born, in the early 1930s, the ranch was hit by a drought. The grass turned brown; with no grass to feed on, the cattle were in danger of starving to death. The *Great Depression* that crippled the nation at this time made things even more difficult.

During her first years on the isolated ranch, Sandra had no other children to play with, but she found plenty of things to entertain her. There was a world of desert and canyons and bluffs to explore and all sorts of wild animals to get to know. Many of the creatures of the desert became Sandra's pets. O'Connor recalled:

One day my father was on a roundup and he found a tiny baby bobcat that had been abandoned by its mother. He put it in his jacket and brought it home. We kept him for years, and he grew up to be a great big gray cat—about four feet long from nose to tail. . . . He acted just like any other cat. He would purr, and cuddle up and sleep a lot.

Eventually, other bobcats came around, and "Bob," as Sandra had named him, went off with them. "Sometimes he would sneak back at night and kill a chicken. One by one the chickens disappeared until they were all gone. After that, Bob came home and stayed for a while, then he disappeared for good."

Sandra tried to tame a desert terrapin (turtle), a raccoon, horned toads, baby coyotes, and a porcupine, without success. She tried to teach crows to speak, with no luck. She had a pet goat, too, but it ate all her mother's plants, so Sandra had to give it away.

One day a little deer appeared at the ranch,

all alone. The deer and Sandra's favorite horse, Chico, became fast friends. "The deer thought he was a horse, and he acted like a horse," recalled Sandra. "Everywhere one went, the other went also."

One of the cowboys found two baby wild javelina pigs and brought them to the house. "We reared them and they got to be very big, and they were very smart. . . . They'd run after someone they liked and follow him around. They were quite interesting pets."

By the age of eight, Sandra was handy with a branding iron, a tractor, and a rifle. She could shoot the critters that attacked the cattle or ate

Ten-year-old Sandra rides her favorite horse, Chico, at the Lazy B ranch. She liked to take Chico on expeditions to the bluffs and canyons on the ranch.

the pasture grass: prairie dogs, coyotes, rattle-snakes, jackrabbits, and Gila monsters. She liked to ride Chico over the hills and plains where creosote bushes, yucca, and broomweed grew. She hoped to be a cattle rancher when she grew up.

Ada Mae shared her love of books with Sandra by reading to her from the *Book of Knowledge* encyclopedia and the newspapers and magazines she received. By the age of four Sandra was able to read books on her own. At night she and her mother would read together by the light of a coal-oil lamp.

Ada Mae wanted her daughter to have a good education, but the nearest school was 30 miles away and was not challenging enough for Sandra. So when Sandra turned six, her parents decided to send her to live with her maternal grandmother, Mamie Scott Wilkey, in El Paso. There Sandra could attend the Radford School for Girls. "We missed her terribly, and she missed us," Ada Mae said later, "but there was no other way for her to get a good education."

Sandra (left) and her cousin Flournoy Davis model matching dresses in 1937. The two girls attended the same school in El Paso, Texas, and became best friends.

3

Expanding Horizons

Mamie Scott Wilkey was firm but kind with Sandra. She had sent her own daughter to college, and she expected the best from her granddaughter, too. Sandra later told an interviewer that Grandmother Wilkey was the strongest influence in her life. "She was a wonderful person—and very supportive of me. She would always tell me that I could do anything I wanted to do. She was convinced of that, and it was very encouraging," said O'Connor.

At Radford, Sandra got to know her cousin, Flournoy Davis, and they became best friends. The two girls spent many summer vacations together at the Lazy B. Sometimes they played with dolls, but most of the time they helped the cowboys with the chores or went exploring on horseback. There was plenty of room to roam—the ranch was five times as big as Washington, D.C. From the top of Round Mountain they could look out over the entire ranch for miles in every direction.

Near the ranch's dry lake beds Sandra and Flournoy discovered Indian artifacts: hollowed-out stones where the Indians had ground their food, and projectile points, often referred to as arrowheads. "Most of the projectile points we found were very small, so they obviously were used to hunt birds or small animals such as rabbits or groundhogs," O'Connor told an interviewer.

The ranch bordered the Gila River, where there was a box canyon. The cousins liked to explore the caves in the canyon's walls, which the

Indians had once used for storage. On the cliffs of the canyon they found pictographs—paintings and drawings done by prehistoric Indians to tell stories.

Each autumn, Sandra and Flournoy said good-bye to the Lazy B ranch and returned to school, but not without a struggle. When it was time to begin the long journey to El Paso, the two girls often hid. "One time," recalled Harry Day, "[they] were swimming in the water tank and refused to come out. I got a lariat and roped them both out of the water. 'Back to school with you girls,' I said."

Sandra worked hard in school and was a top student. Looking back on her school years, O'Connor advises young students "to do the best job you possibly can on every assignment you're given. . . . People will take notice of that, and it becomes a habit to do well. And that will lead to all kinds of opportunities as you grow older."

In 1938, when Sandra was eight years old, her sister, Ann, was born. A year later, her brother, Alan, arrived. Leaving her young siblings behind at the end of each vacation was difficult for Sandra. With each passing year, she missed her family more. When she was in eighth grade, she talked her parents into letting her stay home and go to school in the town of Lordsburg, which was about 30 miles away.

Each weekday morning, her parents had to drive her eight miles on a dusty road to the

Cowboys at the Lazy B ranch brand cattle in 1939. Ranch owners marked their cows to keep cattle rustlers from stealing them to sell elsewhere.

highway, where the school bus would pick her up. Sandra hated the long hours of travel, and the next year she returned to school in El Paso. She would remember the commute years later, when she opposed a law that forced children to take long bus rides to schools in other neighborhoods as a means of making schools racially balanced.

Returning to school in El Paso was not a perfect solution, however. Sandra later admitted that she was often homesick during those years.

As the profits of the ranch increased, the Days were able to travel in the summertime. Over the years they went to such places as Alaska, Cuba, Honduras, and Mexico. One summer the family drove to every state capital west of the Mississippi River.

Sandra enjoyed being the big sister and was sometimes a little bossy with Ann and Alan. Once she caught her brother smoking a cigarette behind a haystack; she delivered such a forceful scolding that he never did that again.

In general, the Day children got along well.

One of their favorite pastimes was listening to the radio. There was no television in those days, so radio programs were an important form of entertainment. Many stories for young people were broadcast. Among Sandra's favorites were "Jack Armstrong, the All-American Boy," and "Grand Central Station."

"I still think radio is the most delightful medium," O'Connor said later. "All kinds of sound effects could give you the idea of what's going on. [The shows] were a lot of fun."

After graduating from Radford at the age of 12, Sandra enrolled at El Paso's Austin High School, where she continued to earn good grades.

"Sandra always knew how to handle herself," one of her high school friends, Hondey Hill McAlmon, recalled later. "She was in honors classes . . . but she also did all the normal things teenagers did—had crushes and talked about boys." Although quiet and a little shy, Sandra was very good at impromptu, or unrehearsed, speaking. This skill would serve her well as a lawyer and a judge.

Sandra graduated from high school when she was only 16 years old and set her sights on Stanford University in Stanford, California. But despite her excellent academic record, her guidance counselor did not think she would be admitted. It was 1946; World War II had recently ended, and millions of veterans from the military were applying for college entrance. Many more men than women were being admitted to the nation's top schools, and Stanford was one of the most competitive. But Sandra was determined to go to Stanford; it was the only university she applied to. Her confidence proved to be well founded. The university's admissions committee accepted her for its 1946 freshman class.

Sandra's father was thrilled. He had intended to go to Stanford himself, but he had had to take over the ranch when his father died. He was happy to see Sandra fulfill his dream.

Twenty-year-old Sandra stands with her mother, Ada Mae, outside their house on the Lazy B ranch. During her years at Stanford University, Sandra often brought friends home during vacations so they could experience the "cowboy" life.

4

Out in the World

Sandra Day was younger than most of the students at Stanford. According to her college roommate, she was easy to get along with and fun to be with, but she was also ambitious and hardworking. At first she studied *economics*, then decided to concentrate on law instead. She enjoyed sorting out the conflicting arguments of a legal case.

Stanford offered an accelerated program that allowed a student to earn both a bachelor's degree (B.A.) and a law degree in six years instead of the usual seven. So, after receiving her B.A.

with high honors in 1950, Sandra went on to Stanford Law School.

Today there may be more women than men in some law schools, but in the 1950s very few women were admitted. When Sandra was a law student at Stanford, the men at the school outnumbered the women 30 to 1.

In law school, students study actual court cases and then must answer detailed questions about them in class—in front of all the other students. This method teaches the students to think quickly under pressure so that they will be able to handle themselves during a real court trial.

Sandra adjusted to the teaching method quickly, studying very hard. She did not want to be caught off guard when the teacher called upon her. She was determined to be prepared in everything she did, a trait that stayed with her. For example, when Sandra was in her forties, she decided to learn to play golf. She took lessons, and every Saturday she went out to a driving range to practice. She did this every week for almost four years before she felt she was ready to play at a golf course. She commented, "I think that anything you do in life requires preparation. And if you are prepared and have thought about it, then things won't be a problem."

At Stanford, Sandra's command of the material and talent for thinking on her feet were rewarded when she was named an editor of the *Stanford Law Review*, a collection of articles on law. The job required many hours of research in the law library. One night at the library she met another student editor, John Jay O'Connor III. Sandra and John dated for the next two years, visiting the Lazy B ranch on several occasions. Her parents liked John, although Harry Day joked later, "I've seen better cowboys."

In the spring of 1952, Sandra graduated third in her law school class. One of the two students who topped her was William Rehnquist, who would later become chief justice of the U.S. Supreme Court.

In December 1952, Sandra and John were

married at the Lazy B ranch. After their wedding the O'Connors returned to California. While John completed his final semester at Stanford, Sandra looked for a job, interviewing at law firms in Los Angeles and San Francisco. Despite her excellent school record, she could not find a firm that would hire her. No law firms had ever hired a female lawyer, and they saw no reason to start.

There seemed to be more opportunities for women in government work, so Sandra made the

Sandra Day (first row, second from left) poses with her Stanford University Law School classmates in 1952. As this photograph illustrates, not many women attended law school at that time.

rounds of county law offices. She took a job as an attorney in the office of the San Mateo county attorney, near Stanford University. She enjoyed the work and decided that her future would be in public service.

When John graduated from law school in June 1953, he was drafted into the army. (The United States was still involved in the Korean War.) He was sent to Frankfurt, West Germany (now called Germany), to work for the army's legal division. Sandra went with him and worked as a lawyer for the Quartermaster Corps, which buys the army's food and equipment and sells surplus supplies. It was her job to check military contracts and to solve any legal problems they presented.

During the O'Connors' three years in Frankfurt, they traveled to many countries in Europe. They also took up skiing, which remains one of their favorite sports.

After returning to the United States in 1956, the couple settled in Phoenix, Arizona, where they could both work as lawyers while being only three hours away from the Days' ranch. But Sandra had to adjust her career plans when she had her first child, Scott, in October 1957. Unable to find a part-time job that would allow her to spend time with Scott, she opened her own law office so that she could have flexible work hours. When her second son, Brian, was born in January 1960, she decided to give up her law practice for a while to be with her children. In May 1962, she gave birth to her third son, Jay.

Sandra intended to return to her career. In the meantime, she stayed involved with the world of law through volunteer work. She also partic-ipated in community activities and worked on behalf of the county Republican party committee. Her husband was also politically active and served on the local planning and zoning commission and hospital advisory board.

In 1965, when Jay was three years old, Sandra obtained a part-time job in the Arizona state attorney general's office. (An attorney general is the chief law officer of a state or the federal government.) Eventually, she worked as an assistant state attorney general on a full-time basis. She remained active in Republican politics, and in 1969 her long hours and dedication to the party were rewarded. She was appointed to fill a vacancy in the Arizona State Senate.

At that time, the world of politics and the law profession were just beginning to open up for women, and they could not have had a more effective trailblazer than Sandra Day O'Connor. As a state senator, she rapidly earned a reputation for being fair and willing to listen to other political points of view. She was also known as a perfectionist who paid attention to the smallest details.

In 1970, O'Connor ran for a full term and won. Two years later, in 1972, she was reelected. That same year, her fellow Republicans chose her as their senate majority leader, and she became the first woman in the nation to serve in that position.

In 1972, Sandra Day O'Connor became the first woman to serve as a state senate majority leader. O'Connor did not feel that she handled the job differently because she was a woman.

5

Judge O'Connor

It was not easy being a senate majority leader. O'Connor had to organize committees, plan ways to pass laws, and unite a group of politicians who had different ideas and interests. She had to be tactful, or polite, but she also had to be tough when it was necessary. One senator she worked with said, "She had a mind like a steel trap. She drove a hard bargain and didn't cave in."

Sandra did not feel that she handled the job differently because she was a woman, but some of the men who worked with her neverthe-less did not always consider her "one of the boys." One committee chairperson, unhappy because he did not get what he wanted, walked up to her and growled, "If you were a man, I'd punch you in the mouth."

Senator O'Connor was not about to let his remark get the better of her. She smiled and said, "If you were a man, you could."

O'Connor carefully read every proposal for new state laws. If the law was one she sup-ported, she made sure every word was the right one and every comma was in place and then worked to persuade the other senators to vote for it. She was unbeatable in a *debate* because she was always the best prepared.

O'Connor's voting record in the Arizona legislature reflected her *conservative* views, but it was impossible to label her as strictly conserva-tive, for she supported a number of *liberal* causes. Among the concerns she championed were *bilin-gual education* and antipollution laws. She also worked for laws to improve job opportunities for women. At the same time, though, she fully supported women who did not choose to work outside the home. She strongly believed in the values of marriage and family.

On the conservative side, she opposed *gun control* and school busing to promote *racial integration*. She also helped write the bill that reinstated the death penalty in Arizona.

Helping to make new laws was exciting, but the study of how the laws actually applied to people's lives remained O'Connor's greatest interest. So, in 1974, she left the state senate to run for election as a trial judge of the Arizona Superior Court, a position that would expose her to "real-life" law. Phoenix had many problems as a result of its rapid growth, and the people wanted a change, so O'Connor easily defeated the judge who had run for reelection.

All kinds of crimes and disputes are settled in trial courts, everything from drug and murder cases to burglaries and divorces. It is the duty of the trial judge to keep the lawyers in line, rule, or decide, on a lawyer's objections to their opponent's tactics, guide the jury (the group of 12 citizens who listen to the evidence and decide whether a *defendant* is innocent or guilty of a crime), and impose *sentences* on the people who are found guilty.

Members of the National Organization for Women demonstrate outside the White House in 1969. Although O'Connor helped pass laws that improved job opportunities for women, she was not active in the women's rights campaign of the 1960s and 1970s.

If Sandra Day O'Connor had been a teacher, she would have been considered a stern but fair one. She would not have put up with any nonsense or accepted any excuses if a student did not do the homework or came to class unprepared. But those who worked hard and did their best would have been graded fairly. That is the

way O'Connor was as a judge. She had no patience with lawyers who had not done the necessary research and paperwork properly or who tried to get by with weak arguments. She did not want her time wasted with a lot of long-winded talk.

Judge O'Connor was tough on criminals, although she found that handing out a sentence was the hardest part of being a judge. For example, in one trial she handled, the mother of 2 young children had been found guilty of passing $3,500 worth of bad checks. The woman begged O'Connor not to give her a sentence that would separate her from her children. As a mother, O'Connor surely understood the woman's anguish. But as a judge, she knew she should not let her own feelings interfere with her decision. She sentenced the woman to 5 to 10 years in prison. When O'Connor announced the sentence, the defendant wailed, "What about my babies?" O'Connor quickly left the courtroom. Alone in her chambers, she burst into tears herself. Sandra later called the decision to jail the woman the toughest she had ever made.

O'Connor's popularity with voters and her record as a judge led the Arizona Republican party to urge her to run for state governor in 1978, against Democrat Bruce Babbitt. After carefully considering the offer, O'Connor decided she would rather remain a judge. The voters elected Babbitt. When there was a vacancy on the Arizona Court of Appeals the next year, O'Connor did not apply for it, but Governor Babbitt nominated her for the position, anyway. She was the best person for the job, he said. O'Connor accepted the offer.

An appeals court is considered a higher, more powerful court than a trial court. Its judges review appeals, or requests, for a rehearing from people who have lost their cases in the lower courts. The judges deal more with papers than with people. Lawyers come before the appeals judges only a few days a week to argue their views on whatever ruling (decision) is in question. The rest of the time the judges read the case records and study the laws and past rulings, then write their *opinions*. The job requires a tremendous amount of reading.

"I encourage young people to learn to become good readers," O'Connor advised. "You need to learn to read quickly and well. It certainly has helped me in every job I've had."

O'Connor enjoyed studying the law and making decisions, and others thought well of her work. She was given high marks by Arizona lawyers for her thoroughness and well-written opinions. She received a slightly lower rating, though, for her personal dealings with attorneys. Some of them did not like her no-nonsense manner.

Despite the demands of her job, O'Connor still found time to do volunteer work. She chaired the board of a museum and actively supported the local public television station.

By this time, John was a member of a large, successful law firm. In addition, he worked for the Legal Aid Society (an organization that offers free legal services to poor people) and other community causes.

In their spare time, John and Sandra played tennis and golf, went skiing, and enjoyed the company of their many friends. They also spent plenty of time with their three sons, who would soon be off to college. The family had a cabin in the mountains of the Lazy B ranch and liked to go there to relax. The cabin was lit by the same kind of coal-oil lamp Sandra had read by as a child. Sandra did not yearn to change her life in any dramatic way.

But on June 17, 1981, Sandra picked up the *Arizona Republic*, a Phoenix newspaper, and read that Supreme Court justice Potter Stewart was retiring. Arizona senator Dennis DeConcini had suggested that President Reagan appoint Sandra Day O'Connor to replace him. By the end of the day, Sandra's telephone was ringing constantly. Her life would never be the same.

O'Connor leaves the Justice Department with Attorney General William French Smith in 1981. For a few years after her appointment to the Supreme Court, the media closely watched and commented on how O'Connor voted in every case.

6

In the Spotlight

The nine individuals who serve as U.S. Supreme Court justices make the final, or supreme, decision about the most important and controversial issues of the country, issues that often directly affect the lives of millions of Americans. Because of the justices' great influence and because they are appointed for life, they are selected very carefully. No one except the president can choose a justice, although the Senate must vote to approve the president's choice. Sometimes there is so much opposition to the person, the Senate rejects the nominee. Then the president has to pick somebody else.

As the president considers who to nominate for an opening on the bench of the Supreme Court, he may ask his attorney general to check if a potential nominee has the work experience necessary to be a qualified candidate. In addition, the Federal Bureau of Investigation (FBI) routinely looks for anything in the nominee's background that might be suspicious or embarrassing if it becomes known publicly.

Judge O'Connor was interviewed by Attorney General William French Smith (who had been a partner in one of the California law firms that had refused to hire her because she was a woman). Afterward, she met with President Reagan, who decided he would look no further; Sandra Day O'Connor was his choice.

According to her son Brian, Sandra remained cool and collected during this time. Even when she received the news that the president had chosen her, she said simply, "Well, let's see what this is all about."

Her biggest challenge was still to come. She

faced days of intense questioning by the Senate Judiciary Committee, which would then make its recommendation to the full Senate. Some Supreme Court nominees' hopes have been wrecked by this committee's direct, often hostile questions. Men of great experience have lost their tempers, fumbled for the right words, and said things they did not mean.

While reporters read the court records to get evidence of her ideas and interviewed just about everyone she had ever known or worked with, O'Connor crammed for the hearings like a high school student facing final exams. She was determined, as always, to be well prepared and to do her best in the bright spotlight of this highly publicized event.

During the confirmation hearings, O'Connor refused to predict how she would vote in cases involving controversial issues, such as the death penalty. This angered some of her critics, who felt that she should be more open about her opinions. She did openly express her confidence in state government, which she believes is better able to deal with problems than federal government because it is closer to the people. Her middle-of-the-road, moderate attitude satisfied neither the nation's very liberal people nor its very conservative people. But her fairness and willingness to consider all sides of a disagreement earned the approval of 17 of the 18 committee members and the entire U.S. Senate.

With President Reagan and the eight black-robed justices looking on, Sandra Day O'Connor was sworn in on September 25, 1981. Her parents, husband, and three sons were also in the courtroom as she repeated the oath that all federal officials, including the president, are required to swear:

I, Sandra Day O'Connor, do solemnly swear that I will support and defend the Constitution of the United States against all enemies, foreign and domestic; that I will bear true faith and allegiance to the same; that I take this obligation freely, without any mental reservation or purpose of evasion; and that I will well and faithfully discharge the duties of the office on which I am about to enter. So help me God.

O'Connor had already sat in on meetings to decide what cases the Court would be hearing during its upcoming session and had begun reading the cases that had been selected.

More than 5,000 petitions are sent to the Supreme Court each year by people who have lost their cases in the lower courts and want them reconsidered. Only 130 to 150 of them will be accepted. The cases must raise difficult questions about federal laws or the U.S. Constitution—the document that outlines the rights of all American citizens. For example, the Constitution guarantees "freedom of speech," but it does not define exactly what that means. So legal arguments about the definition often arise.

Suppose, for instance, someone goes around telling lies about another person. People believe the lies, and nobody will associate with that person anymore. Should the one telling the lies be punished, or is he or she protected by the right of free speech? Or suppose a student writes an article for the school newspaper criticizing the principal, and the teacher in charge of the paper

refuses to let it be printed. Does the school have the authority to censor what is in the school paper? These are the kinds of questions for which the Supreme Court provides the final decision.

One of the most important opinions Justice O'Connor wrote in her first term was a de-

Proudly flanking the newly appointed justice are (from left) Harry Day, John O'Connor, Ada Mae Day, Chief Justice Warren Burger, and Brian, Jay, and Scott O'Connor.

55

cision that said an all-female school of nursing in Mississippi could not keep out men who wanted to be nurses. The Court was divided 4–4 on the question; O'Connor's vote tipped the balance. She did not think men were being treated fairly in this case.

Because she is willing to consider all arguments, she sometimes votes with the more liberal justices—as she did in the nursing school case—and other times with the more conservative judges. Her "swing vote," which is less predictable than the other judges' votes and often determines the Court's final decision, makes her seem to be the most powerful woman in the country.

For a few years after her appointment, reporters focused on how Justice O'Connor voted in every case. Her positions were analyzed far more than the opinions of the other judges. "That media scrutiny . . . [was something] I would have preferred was not there, but it certainly did not affect the way I did my job."

The work O'Connor does as a Supreme

Court justice is similar to the work she had done as an appeals judge in Arizona, although she has to work longer hours. She said:

> I do a lot of homework. To decide a case, I have to read all the briefs [the written summary of a case] that are filed by the parties. And briefs aren't brief at all; they're long. And there are many of them. It's a little like solving a difficult puzzle. And then we have to be able to express our opinions in writing. We try to write clearly and well, so that everyone around the country can read and understand what we've said.

It would take a while for O'Connor to learn the ropes, to get to know the other justices, and to feel confident in questioning attorneys during their oral, or spoken, arguments. When the Court adjourned for the summer after her first term, her family noticed that Justice O'Connor looked tired. This was something new for the wife and mother whose energy had always seemed endless.

Justice Sandra Day O'Connor poses for an official portrait in 1991. O'Connor urges more women to become involved in government and expects that the time will come when she will no longer be the only female judge on the Supreme Court.

7
Personal Challenges

For the three O'Connor sons, their mother's high position was nothing new. "When they were young," Justice O'Connor explained, "I had a succession of jobs that were unusual for [a woman to hold] . . . majority leader of the legislature, trial court judge, appellate court judge, and I think they took it very much for granted that their mother was in some such position and they didn't think anything of it, and I'm not sure if that attitude has changed since I have been here."

By the start of her second term in 1982, Sandra Day O'Connor had settled into the job. She had become bolder in getting other justices to agree with her, and she even enjoyed the challenge of it: "To persuade other justices that you are correct is an exciting part of the job," commented O'Connor. By the second term, she was also aiming sharp questions at the lawyers, just as she had done as a trial court judge.

In some respects, her husband had the biggest adjustment to make in moving to Washington. He had had to leave his successful law practice in Phoenix and start over again. The press often asked him if he felt overshadowed by his wife's impressive position. He said that he did not mind at all; he was very proud of her success.

John joined a Washington law firm, and he and Sandra were welcomed into Washington society. They were invited to many parties, and they liked to dance. John also enjoys telling jokes, which he collects in notebooks that now fill a shelf in his library.

The O'Connors became members of a country club, where Sandra continues to play golf and tennis at least once a week. She believes that physical fitness is important for mental fitness. "I am more productive when I feel good physically," she said. One of the first things she did when she joined the Court was to start a daily exercise class for the women who work in the Court building. The class was readily accepted by the Court's female employees, although it caused a commotion among the males. One justice commented that "it took some getting used to, seeing those black leotarded ladies in the halls of the Court."

Justice O'Connor is demanding of the people who work for her, but no more than she is of herself. She can get by on four hours of sleep; she expects her four law clerks to work long hours.

Because it is a tradition that federal law clerks work for one year only, Sandra has to hire new ones every year. She studies more than 100 applications, then interviews 10 or 12 finalists, all of whom are top graduates of leading law schools. It is an honor to be selected to clerk for a Supreme Court justice, and it is also a big boost to a young lawyer's career.

Among other things, O'Connor strives to teach her clerks the importance of paying attention to detail. For example, when the clerks draft opinions for her, she asks them to wheel a library book cart into her office loaded with all the material they used to research the case. She insists on reviewing everything they have cited for herself. If she finds mistakes in their work, she does not hesitate to point them out.

O'Connor is considerate of her employees and appreciates their efforts. When they work on Saturdays, she often brings Mexican food for everyone. Each year, she takes her staff on a local outing, going to such places as the National Arboretum, the Folger Shakespeare Library, or the Smithsonian Institution.

At the end of each term she treats her departing clerks to an adventurous trip. One year they all went white-water rafting on a river in Pennsylvania. The guide insisted that no one leave the raft even if somebody fell overboard. But when Justice O'Connor was swept into the river, all the clerks ignored the rules and jumped in after her. As it turned out, she saved herself with little effort. The clerks were scolded by the raft guide, who was furious that his instructions had been disobeyed. Even so, one of the clerks commented: "If you are clerking for Sandra Day O'Connor, you aren't going to be the one to let her drown. Her other clerks, and a few million other people besides, would never forgive you!"

Sandra has given parties for her former law clerks and their families. For all her reserve, she is thought of as a warm, considerate person by those who know her best.

O'Connor receives hundreds of letters every day. In the months following her Supreme Court appointment, most of the letters were from women who appreciated her pioneering achievements and felt her success had inspired their own careers. O'Connor had not been active in the women's rights campaign of the 1960s and 1970s, but she admits that without the *feminists'* fight for greater opportunities for women, she "would not be serving in this job."

As time went on, she began to receive letters from people urging her to vote this way or that way on matters before the Court. These she ignores. Many children send her letters in which they ask what it is like to be the only "girl judge" on the Supreme Court.

O'Connor is often asked to give speeches at college graduations and at various organizations. She also swears in other government officials. In the fall of 1989, O'Connor had the pleasure of taking part in a particularly special ceremony. She swore in one of her former law clerks, Ruth MacGregor, as a judge on the same Arizona Court of Appeals bench she had once occupied herself. In order to meet these commitments, O'Connor has to organize her time for months ahead.

Sandra Day O'Connor's experience on the Supreme Court has deepened her belief that all U.S. citizens should understand the meaning of the Constitution in order to make sure that its ideals are upheld. She said:

> Our Constitution was not intended solely, or even primarily, for judges. The strength of our freedoms depends on how firmly [these freedoms] stand in the hearts of our citizens. Without an educational structure which fosters and encourages each successive group of students to learn about the structure of our government and the history of its development, we would soon see young hearts barren of those sentiments and understandings out of which our nation came into existence.

O'Connor has faced personal challenges since she became a Supreme Court justice. Three years after she took office, her father died at age 86. In the autumn of 1988, O'Connor, then 58, learned that she had breast cancer. She later told friends that the two weeks that followed the diagnosis were the worst of her life. Living with such uncertainty was a new experience for her. But as she had done with many things in her life, she decided her best defense was to be well prepared. Before deciding on her course of treatment, she talked to breast cancer experts and read everything she could find on the subject. Then her surgery was scheduled, which would be followed by chemotherapy. Checking her calendar, she discovered that she had accepted an invitation to speak at Washington and Lee University in Lexington, Virginia, on the day before the surgery. Courageously, she made the three-and-a-half-hour drive to Lexington, gave the speech, then returned to Washington and checked into the hospital.

A few weeks later she was playing golf and tennis again and did not miss a single hearing before the Court. In the midst of her chemotherapy treatment, she did confess to feeling a little tired. "Welcome to the human race," John O'Connor said affectionately.

That Christmas, Sandra's favorite present was a set of rain gear, which she planned to wear on the golf course. Commenting on his mother's strong spirit and drive, Scott said, "She's not going to let a little thing like rain get in the way."

The following year, in April 1989, Sandra's mother died at the age of 85. With tears in her eyes, Sandra led the family service atop Round Mountain, overlooking the Lazy B ranch. Her sister, Ann, who is a state senator in Arizona, and her brother, Alan, who manages the ranch, joined Sandra in scattering their mother's ashes along the mountaintop.

The year ended on a happier note: In October she welcomed her first grandchild, a girl named Courtney Day O'Connor, born to Scott and his wife. A photo of the baby soon found its way to her desk.

In 1990, O'Connor and the other justices decided a case that is important to students all over the nation. The case grew out of a disagreement between a high school student in Omaha,

Nebraska, and school officials. The student asked permission to start a Christian club for classmates who wanted to study the Bible and pray together. The club would meet at the school, after school hours, just as the school's other groups—math, choir, chess, and others—did. But the school board said they could not allow a Christian club to meet at the school. They felt that if they allowed the club to meet it would suggest to people that the high school was endorsing, or supporting, a particular religion, and it was against the law for a federally funded public school to do that. The student insisted it was unconstitutional for the school to deny her request, and she filed a lawsuit.

When the case reached the Supreme Court, the justices decided in favor of the high school student. O'Connor, who wrote an opinion for the Court, said that because the Christian club would be meeting after school hours and would not involve teachers, it would not cause students to think the school was favoring a religion. O'Connor also pointed out that high school students are old enough to know that the school is not pressuring them to join the club, that it is just one of many activities they are free to participate in if they wish. Eight of the nine justices voted in favor of the student's right to form a Christian club; it was a fairly easy decision.

Another 1990 Supreme Court case sparked more disagreement among the justices and among people all over the nation. The Supreme Court justices were asked to decide whether a new law passed by Congress, called the Flag Protection Act, violated the Constitution. The law would have made it a crime for anyone to burn, mutilate, or trample upon the American flag in public. (The law was created in response to a 1989 Supreme Court decision that declared a Texas law against flag burning unconstitutional. The Texas law had been challenged by a man who had been arrested for burning a flag as a part of a political protest.)

Many people in the country, including President George Bush, supported the Flag Protection Act. They felt that the American flag should not be treated disrespectfully. But many others did not think the law was fair because it violated a citizen's constitutional right to express his or her ideas freely. Five of the Supreme Court justices agreed with this second view, believing that it is the right to protest, even when it is offensive, that makes our nation different from the rest of the world. Because they formed the majority—meaning more justices were against the new law than for it—the Flag Protection Act was struck down.

O'Connor was among the four justices who thought the new law should be upheld. She and the others argued that the American flag's unique position as a symbol of our nation justified a law forbidding people from harming it. One justice argued that the law did not interfere with the right to free speech, because it did not stop a person from criticizing the flag and the nation it represents in other ways, such as through speeches.

Naturally, O'Connor wished the Court had upheld the law, but she is not one to dwell on decisions once they have been made and does not spend time wondering whether she voted correctly. As she once told an interviewer, "I try to do the best job I can and never look back."

Sandra Day O'Connor's office is decorated with objects from the landscape that helped shape her. American Indian baskets, pottery, and paintings of Indian scenes adorn her walls and shelves. A large chunk of colorful petrified wood sits on the fireplace mantel. She says her favorite colors are the soft peachlike tones of the desert. On the little finger of her right hand she wears a ring made from a piece of turquoise that had been found in an old copper pit near the Lazy B. "It's not particularly good quality turquoise," she said, "but it came from my part of the country." A tall woman, Sandra Day O'Connor speaks quietly, thoughtfully measuring her words. Her square, sturdy hands look as though they can still handle the reins of a horse or mend a fence.

O'Connor accepts that she is a role model. She views her position on the Supreme Court as a sign that there are unlimited opportunities for women today. She urges more women to get involved in government and expects the time will come when she will no longer be the only woman judge on the Supreme Court.

Frances Perkins, who became the first woman member of the *cabinet* as secretary of labor in 1933, often said, "I had been taught long ago by my grandmother that if anybody opens a door, one should always go through."

When a door opened for Sandra Day O'Connor, she, too, went through. She hopes that the girls and boys who read her story will be inspired to do the same.

Further Reading

Other Biographies of Sandra Day O'Connor

Bentley, Judith. *Justice Sandra Day O'Connor*. New York: Messner, 1983.

Fox, Mary Virginia. *Justice Sandra Day O'Connor*. Hillside, NJ: Enslow, 1983.

Woods, Harold, and Geraldine Woods. *Equal Justice: A Biography of Sandra Day O'Connor*. Minneapolis: Dillon Press, 1985.

Related Books

Hoopes, Roy. *What the United States Senator Does*. New York: HarperCollins, 1975.

Johnson, Joan. *Justice*. New York: Watts, 1985.

Morris, Richard B. *The Constitution*. Minneapolis: Lerner, 1985.

Chronology

March 26, 1930	Born Sandra Day in El Paso, Texas, she spends her childhood at her family's Lazy B ranch on the Arizona–New Mexico border.
1946	Sandra graduates from high school in El Paso.
1950	Sandra graduates with honors from Stanford University.
1952	Sandra graduates from Stanford University Law School; she marries John Jay O'Connor III; she becomes deputy county attorney in San Mateo, California.
1953	Sandra Day O'Connor accepts a job as a lawyer in Frankfurt, West Germany.
1956	The O'Connors return from Europe and settle in Phoenix, Arizona.
1957	After giving birth to the first of three sons, O'Connor opens a law practice.

1965	O'Connor becomes an Arizona assistant attorney general.
1969	O'Connor is appointed to the Arizona State Senate.
1970	O'Connor is elected to the Arizona State Senate.
1972	O'Connor becomes the state senate majority leader.
1974	O'Connor is elected judge of the Arizona Superior Court.
1979	O'Connor is appointed as a judge to the Arizona Court of Appeals.
1981	O'Connor is appointed to the U.S. Supreme Court, becoming America's first female Supreme Court justice.
1984	O'Connor's father dies.
1988	O'Connor undergoes treatment for breast cancer.
1989	O'Connor's mother dies.
1990	O'Connor writes the opinion for the Supreme Court decision that grants a Nebraska student the right to form a Christian club at her high school; she votes in favor of the Flag Protection Act, but the law is struck down.

Glossary

bilingual education   a system of teaching in the United States in which minority students with little knowledge of English are taught in their native language

cabinet   the group of people chosen by the U.S. president to head the federal government's executive departments and to act as official advisers to the president

conservative   having political or social views that favor the way things are and distrust changes or reforms

debate   a discussion of the reasons for and against something

defendant   a person accused of a crime

economics   the science that deals with the development and use of money, goods, and services

feminist   a person who believes that women should have the same political, social, and economic rights as men

Great Depression   the period of severe economic collapse and joblessness in the United States in the 1930s

gun control   a policy of strict regulation of the buying and selling of guns

legislature   a body of people with the power to make and change laws for a state or a nation

liberal   having political or social views that favor change and reform

majority leader   the leader of the political party that has the most people in a lawmaking body, such as the **U.S. Senate** or House of Representatives

opinion   a written explanation of the legal reasons on which a court decision is based

racial integration   the policy of ending racial **segregation**   by bringing people of different races together, as in a school system

segregation   the policy of keeping people of different races separate, as in schools, housing, and industry

sentence   the judge's decision about what punishment to give a person found guilty of a crime

unconstitutional   not in agreement with the principles outlined in the Constitution of the United States

U.S. Senate   one of the two houses of Congress, to which two members are elected from each state by popular vote for a six-year term; the other is the U.S. House of Representatives

Index

Norman L. Macht holds a bachelor of philosophy degree from the University of Chicago and received a master's degree in political science from Sonoma State University. He writes extensively on finance and sports history and is the author of several biographies in the Chelsea House BASEBALL LEGENDS series. In addition, Macht has written a biography of Christopher Columbus for the Chelsea House JUNIOR WORLD BIOGRAPHIES series. He is currently working on a biography of the American sportsman Connie Mack and is founder and president of a features syndicate based in Newark, Delaware.

Picture Credits